One for All

A Pennslyvania Number Book

Written by Trinka Hakes Noble and Illustrated by L.W. Papp

Text Copyright © 2005 Trinka Hakes Noble
Illustration Copyright © 2005 Lisa Papp

Sleeping Bear Press

310 North Main Street, Suite 300
Chelsea, MI 48118
www.sleepingbearpress.com

THOMSON
GALE

© 2005 Thomson Gale, a part of the Thomson Corporation.

Thomson, Star Logo and Sleeping Bear Press are trademarks and Gale is a registered trademark used herein under license.

Printed and bound in Canada.

10 9 8 7 6 5 4 3 2 1

Library of Congress Cataloging-in-Publication Data

Noble, Trinka Hakes.
One for all : a Pennsylvania number book / written by Trinka Hakes Noble; illustrated by Lisa Papp.
p. cm.
Summary: "Using numbers many of Pennsylvania's state symbols, history, land-scapes, and famous people are introduced. Topics include the Liberty Bell, fireflies, Gettysburg, Betsy Ross, and coal miners"—Provided by publisher.
ISBN 1-58536-200-X
1. Pennsylvania—Juvenile literature. 2. Counting—Juvenile literature. I. Papp, Lisa, ill. II. Title.

F149.3.N63 2005
974.8—dc22   2005007467

For The RiverStone Writers—

Denise, Elvira, Joyce, Pam, Pat, and Sally—
who can always count on each other.

T.H.N.

❧

With heartfelt thanks to Trinka and Sleeping Bear Press.

LISA

Hurry, hurry! Don't be late.
You've got a Keystone counting date,
to count these numbers from small to great.
Let's enumerate the Keystone State!

The Liberty Bell is one of our nation's most precious treasures, with its Biblical inscription: "Proclaim Liberty throughout all the land, unto all the inhabitants thereof."

The bell was cast in England in 1751 to commemorate the 50th anniversary of William Penn's Charter of Privileges, which he granted his colony of Pennsylvania in 1701. However, the bell cracked shortly after it was shipped to Philadelphia and local craftsmen recast it.

The Declaration of Independence, penned by Thomas Jefferson, was adopted on July 4, 1776 and at noon on July 8th the Liberty Bell rang across the city, calling all its citizens to the first public reading. In 1777 the bell was secreted out of Philadelphia and hidden in Allentown for safekeeping from the invading British.

Today the Liberty Bell safely resides in the glass Liberty Bell Center in Philadelphia, the "city of brotherly love."

one
1

Our Liberty Bell is number 1,
announcing the birth of our nation.
It rang from Independence Hall so high,
in 1776, in the month of July.

In the 1830s canals linked Pennsylvania's major rivers. By 1840 one thousand miles of canals were in use, more than in any other state.

Canal boats carried both freight and passengers. Two mules towed the boat along at two or three miles an hour. Bridges over the canals were low, so passengers riding on top had to duck or lie flat. Canal boatmen and their families lived on the boats. A young boy was hired to walk with the mules on the towpath and keep them moving.

In Pennsylvania canal boats were built in two sections for easy turning in narrow canals. They were also taken apart, loaded on the Allegheny Portage Railroad, and hauled over the Appalachian Divide to continue traveling. Today, in New Hope, you can still enjoy a tranquil canal boat ride pulled by mules along the Delaware River, and in Easton you can tour the National Canal Museum.

two

2

2 lanky brown mules working in a pair,
pull a canal boat up the Delaware.
Steady on the towpath til the sun goes down,
dreaming of their stable back in Easton town.

Heinz Field

Allegheny River

Ohio River

Point State Park

Monongahela River

In Pittsburgh we find our number 3,
the Ohio, Monongahela, and Allegheny.
Three mighty rivers carve through the landscape
Pittsburgh's Golden Triangle, a three-sided shape.

Pittsburgh was founded at the point where the Allegheny and Monongahela Rivers join to form the mighty Ohio River. Both the French and the British wanted this strategic point. In 1758 the British gained control and built Fort William Pitt where Point State Park is today. This is how Pittsburgh got its name.

The nation's first commercial steamboat, the *New Orleans* (built by Robert Fulton), was launched on the banks of the Monongahela River in 1811. This made Pittsburgh a major inland port, and when the first railroad was completed in 1852, many immigrants moved in to form close-knit neighborhoods.

Pittsburgh grew into a major industrial center, with famous industrialists such as Andrew Carnegie for steel and Henry J. Heinz for processed foods. Today Pittsburgh is enjoying a renaissance with a revitalized downtown called the Golden Triangle.

three

3

The Pennsylvania Turnpike was our nation's first high-speed, multilane highway. When it opened in 1940 there was no fixed speed limit.

The first major road in Pennsylvania was constructed in 1677, named the King's Path. In 1794 a 69-mile stone-surfaced road was built from Philadelphia to Lancaster at great expense. Travelers had to paid a toll collected at gates, or pikes, which were long poles across the road, and then the pike would be turned to let travelers pass. That is why toll roads are called turnpikes today.

The oldest tunnel for public use was dug in 1832 near Lebanon. At that time, "tunnel" was a new word to many Americans. The four tunnels on the Pennsylvania Turnpike today are the Allegheny, the Tuscarora, the Kittatinny, and the Blue Mountain.

Pennsylvania has the nation's fourth largest highway system, which includes 55,000 bridges and over 110,000 miles of roads. Each year over 172.8 million vehicles use the turnpike.

four
4

On Pennsylvania's Turnpike, let's take a ride
on our first multilane highway nationwide.
4 tunnels open just like a door,
so you can drive through a mountain's core.

In 1681 William Penn founded Pennsylvania based on his Quaker faith, where all could worship freely. Many English Quakers followed. Soon, smaller German sects seeking religious freedom came—Mennonites, Amish, German Quakers, and Moravians. These Pennsylvania Germans lived in close farming communities with strong religious and family ties. Because of their simple and traditional ways, they became known as the Plain Sects or Plain People.

Of the Plain People, the Amish are the strictest. They do not have cars, phones, or electricity, and keep to their separate ways, living mainly in Lancaster, York, and Berks Counties.

Most Amish are farmers but many are also fine craftsmen. However, items made by the Amish will have a small imperfection because only God can make it perfect. Amish women use solid colors in their quilts because prints, plaids, and calicos are considered "too fancy" and worldly. For the Amish, a quilt's primary purpose is for warmth.

five

5

5 Amish quilts in colors so bold,
hang on a clothesline, waiting to be sold.
Three are brand new and two are very old,
but all will keep us warm on nights so cold.

In Conestoga Valley the Germans invented the mighty Conestoga wagon in the mid-1700s. By 1775 wagon trains of 50 to 100 traveled the Old Lancaster Road and Reading Pike to Philadelphia, averaging 15 miles a day. They hauled between four and eight tons of freight, everything from farm products to linens to iron ore.

These wagons were drawn by six draft horses, a special American breed also called the Conestoga. At 17 hands high and weighing 1,600 lb., each horse wore brass bells that chimed on a hoop above their harnesses. Six huge horses and a fully loaded wagon measured an impressive 60 feet in length. To pass lesser vehicles, the wagoners began driving on the right, and that is why today America drives on the right side of the road.

By 1830 three thousand wagons a day were on the road from Philadelphia to Pittsburgh, hauling freight, traders, and settlers. You can see a real Conestoga wagon at the Landis Valley Museum near Lancaster.

six

6

6 mighty horses, all day long,
pull a Conestoga wagon, steady and strong.
Down to Philadelphia and all the way back,
never getting stuck in the muddy track.

Runaway slaves kept 7 stars in sight.
The Big Dipper led them north through the night.
The Underground Railroad helped them to hide,
in Pennsylvania's safe countryside.

In 1780 Pennsylvania became the first state to abolish slavery. Quakers and free blacks started a secret system around 1800 called the Underground Railroad to help runaway slaves flee north to Canada. Escaping after dark, runaways used the stars as a map. The Big Dipper, which they called "the drinking gourd," lines up with the North Star, which pointed them north.

Dividing the north and south, the Mason-Dixon Line is the southern border of Pennsylvania. Once runaways crossed into Pennsylvania, they searched for Underground Railroad guides called "conductors." The conductors guided slaves to "stations" or safe houses where they were hidden and given food and shelter. Often one light in a window signaled that it was a safe house. This was dangerous because the Fugitive Slave Law made it a crime to help runaway slaves, and bounty hunters stalked the routes north.

Over 3,200 workers on the Underground Railroad helped 100,000 slaves to freedom.

seven
7

8 bright colors sit on a palette,
   waiting for the brush of an artist's talent,
to paint Penn's Woods for all the world to see,
   its valleys green and hills serene in splendid beauty.

The first art museum and art school in America, the Pennsylvania Academy of Fine Arts, was founded in Philadelphia in 1805. Pittsburgh native Mary Cassatt studied at the art academy before moving to Paris and becoming an Impressionist painter. Modern artist Andy Warhol started the Pop Art movement in the 1970s. His works are displayed in the Andy Warhol Museum in Pittsburgh.

Today the best-known Pennsylvanian painters are the Wyeth family. N.C. Wyeth was a great illustrator, known for his illustrations of *Treasure Island*. His son, Andrew Wyeth, is world renowned for his paintings of Pennsylvania and Maine, capturing the essence of both places. Jamie Wyeth is following in the footsteps of his grandfather and father, and is an acclaimed painter in his own right. Paintings by the Wyeth clan, which includes the largest collection of Andrew Wyeth's paintings, can be seen at the Brandywine River Museum in Chadds Ford.

eight
8

Little League Baseball began in Williamsport.
Now kids worldwide play this American sport.
So **9** young players whether big, short, or tall,
play nine innings long when the ump yells "**PLAY BALL!**"

Born in 1752, Betsy Ross was the eighth child in a Philadelphia Quaker family of 17 children. She lost two husbands to the cause of independence, but managed to care for her daughters and run an upholstery shop and sewing business on Arch Street. Besides furniture upholstery, she made bed hangings, sheets and linens, soldier's uniforms, ship pennants, and was the official flag maker for the Pennsylvania Navy.

Historians do not know for sure that Betsy Ross made the first American flag. But legend has it that one day in 1776, a committee from the Continental Congress—George Washington, Robert Morris, and George Ross—secretly came to her shop and commissioned Betsy Ross to create a new flag for the colonies.

On June 14, 1777, the Congress officially adopted Betsy Ross's design, stating "the flag of the United States be thirteen stripes, alternate red and white; that the union be thirteen stars, white in a field of blue, representing a new constellation."

thirteen
13

Betsy Ross made, with needle, thread, and thimble,
13 our country's first flag, an American symbol.
By sewing stars in a circle on blue,
our colonies united into a nation so new.

Pennsylvania has 45,000 miles of rivers and streams. The brook trout is the official state fish. There are more than 150 species of fish in the state, including all six species of pike.

Pennsylvania has over 200 covered bridges, more than any other state. They are covered for protection from winter's snow and ice, and are nostalgically called "kissin' bridges."

The firefly is the state insect. Their glow is produced by a chemical reaction in a light organ located on their underside, warning their predators that they taste bitter. Frogs eat them anyway, and maybe a hungry brook trout would, too. But to Pennsylvanians, the glimmer of fireflies adds a magical touch to a summer evening.

fourteen

14

14 fireflies shimmer, glimmer, and gleam,
hovering above a Pennsylvania stream.
Along swims a brook trout with a hungry look,
but from a covered bridge drops a fishing hook!

Pennsylvania means "Penn's Woods." In 1681 King Charles II granted the land to William Penn, and it was named in honor of Penn's father. The wooded hills are a perfect habitat for white-tailed deer, which is the official state animal. The ruffed grouse, an upland game bird, is Pennsylvania's state bird. Sixty percent of Pennsylvania is covered by forest.

The hemlock pine is the state tree. Over a century ago, the hemlock and white pine played an important role in the state lumber industry because they were in great demand for shipbuilding. Lumbermen cut the trees, tied them into log rafts, and floated them downriver to be exported to England's shipyards. You can visit a logging camp at the Pennsylvania Lumber Museum in Galeton. In northeastern Pennsylvania, the Woodbourne Forest and Wildlife Sanctuary contains 150 acres of virgin woods with some trees estimated to be 800 years old. Pennsylvania still lives up to its name–Penn's Woods.

fifteen
15

15 hemlocks in a shady glen,
shelter the chicks of a ruffed grouse hen.
Suddenly a deer bounds through the glen and then,
all is peaceful in the woods of William Penn.

Benjamin Franklin is legendary.
He founded the first public library.
So **20** great books are yours to borrow.
Just bring them back two weeks from tomorrow!

Benjamin Franklin is one of the most loved figures in American history. Born into a poor Boston family in 1706, he moved to Philadelphia as a young man in 1723. In Philadelphia he founded the first circulating library in the world. He was a printer, editor, publisher, and author, best known for the popular *Poor Richard's Almanac.* As a gifted scientist, he invented the lightning rod, bifocal glasses, and the cast iron Franklin stove.

But above all, Benjamin Franklin is best remembered as a patriot. He both shaped and signed the Declaration of Independence and the Constitution of the United States. In his seventies, Franklin became a diplomat to France, securing French support for the American Revolution.

Andrew Carnegie is another Pennsylvanian who cared about libraries. Through the Carnegie Corporation he established 2,509 libraries throughout the United States and English-speaking world, many of which are still in use today.

twenty
20

Fred Rogers was the host of the Emmy Award-winning children's program– *Mister Rogers' Neighborhood*. It was the longest running television program in Public Broadcasting history. Fred Rogers, born in 1928 in Latrobe, was a longtime resident of Pittsburgh, a city that revered him. His children's show was inspired by the friendly and unique neighborhoods of Pittsburgh, including the "neighborhood trolley," the library, the bakery, and many of its friendly characters. It was produced there from 1968 to 2001.

In 2002 Fred Rogers was presented the Medal of Freedom from President Bush and received a star on the Hollywood Walk of Fame. Fred Rogers died in February 2003 but will be fondly remembered by millions of children who visited *Mister Rogers' Neighborhood* each day.

thirty
30

Fred Rogers is known for his kind, gentle way,
and the cardigan sweaters he wore each day.
So counting **30** sweaters would be good,
to honor *Mister Rogers' Neighborhood.*

40 twisty Slinkys™ flip and bend,
toppling downstairs, end over end.
Quick, can you count them as they descend?
You can if you count by 5s and 10s!

Ever since Benjamin Franklin's famous electrical experiment in 1752, our state has been noted for inventions and discoveries. Joseph Priestly, considered the founder of modern chemistry, discovered oxygen in 1774. Our country's first medical school opened in 1765 at the College and Academy of Philadelphia, now the University of Pennsylvania. At the University of Pittsburgh, Dr. Jonas Salk discovered the polio vaccine.

The Slinky™ is part toy and part engineering marvel. In 1943 Richard James invented the Slinky™ while working on a spring that would keep ship's instruments steady at sea.

In Philadelphia in 1858, Hyman L. Lipman gave us the practical invention of a pencil with an attached eraser, and E. Irvin and Clarence Scott invented the paper towel in 1907. Some inventions are good enough to eat! The banana split was invented in Latrobe in 1904 and Harry B. Reese of York County concocted the Reese's Peanut Butter Cup™ in 1923.

50 happy tubers bob down the Delaware,
on a lazy summer day without a care.
Splashing and laughing in groups of 10.
Count them as they float 'round the bend.

The Delaware River is the eastern border of Pennsylvania and is the only East Coast waterway that has not been dammed. In the summer its shallow and slow-moving waters make it perfect for riding inner tubes, canoeing, and swimming. The spectacular Delaware Water Gap, with dramatic 1,000-foot cliffs, opens up into the beautiful Pocono Mountains, which have the largest Environmental Learning Center in the Western Hemisphere.

The Pine Creek Gorge Natural Area is in Tioga State Forest and could be called the "Grand Canyon" of Pennsylvania. This 45-mile-long gorge with its fast-moving Pine Creek attracts kayakers and white-water rafters, along with campers and hikers. Pennsylvania has numerous trails, which include 230 miles of the Appalachian Trail.

Some of Pennsylvania's water attractions are man-made. At Dorney Park & Wildwater Kingdom near Allentown is one of the tallest waterfall slides in the world.

fifty
50

60 coal miners, each one a Pennsylvanian,
　　　deep underground, they work subterranean.
　　　So 60 hard hats need lights so bright,
because coal tunnels are black as midnight.

Deep beneath the mountains of Pennsylvania, prehistoric swamps were compressed into the largest deposit of anthracite coal, or hard coal, in the world. Hard coal burned hot with less smoke and was called "black diamonds." All of our nation's hard coal comes from Pennsylvania. It fueled the Civil War, Pittsburgh's steel industry, and our state's growing railroads.

But working in a coal mine was dangerous. Many miners were immigrants, working long hours in poor conditions for low pay. Many children had to work, too. Boys as young as eight worked in unheated sheds next to the mines, picking out pieces of shale from the coal. When a boy turned 12, he worked in the mines with his father. Miners and their families suffered many hardships living in company towns where a single company owned all the houses, schools, and stores. Eckley Miners' Village, settled in 1854, is a restored coal town, which preserves the difficult life of coal miners and their families, yet pays homage to the pride and spirit that bonded them together.

sixty
60

About 12,000 years ago the first people in Pennsylvania were hunter-gatherers. Later they became hunter-farmers, clearing land, planting crops, and building permanent villages of bark and mud houses along rivers.

The Lenni Lenape, which means the "ordinary people" or "common people," lived in the east along both sides of the Delaware River and were a peace-loving people. They spoke an Algonquian language similar to most Northeastern woodland tribes, and Europeans referred to them as the Delaware. The Susquehannak, or "people of the well-watered land," lived along the Susquehanna River and spoke Iroquois. They built villages of "long houses." The Monongahela built their villages on hilltops enclosed with a strong log fence. The Erie lived along the southern shore of Lake Erie, and the Huron and Shawnee lived in the Ohio Valley.

Unfortunately, in the 1600s attacks from the powerful Iroquois and diseases from European settlers greatly diminished the Native population.

seventy

70

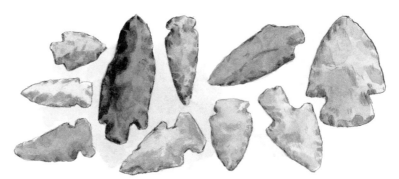

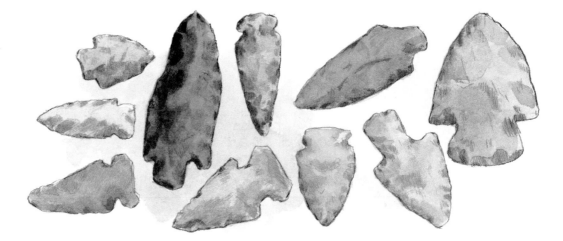

The Lenni Lenape long ago lived here,
hunting and fishing with bow, arrow, and spear.
70 What a special treasure it would be to find
arrowheads they left behind.

80 Crayola® crayons should do the trick,
with every color from which to pick,
so you can create your very own designs
and you don't have to stay inside the lines!

Cousins Edwin Binney and C. Harold Smith introduced the Crayola® crayon. Their first box of crayons was produced in 1903 and cost a nickel. It contained eight colors—red, orange, yellow, green, blue, violet, brown, and black. The word Crayola is a combination of the French word *craie* meaning "chalk," and the English word *oleaginous*, which means "oily." Crayons are a mixture of melted wax and pure powdered color.

In 1996 The Crayola FACTORY®, a family-oriented, hands-on discovery center where you can see how Crayola crayons and markers are made, was built in downtown Easton. In 2003, The Crayola FACTORY went through an expansion, adding two Animation Stations and a theater to the many creative and artistic activities for visitors eager to try their artistic hand. Since it opened in 1996, The Crayola FACTORY has entertained more than 2.5 million visitors from all over the world.

eighty

80

Pretzel is a German word but it originated from the Latin word *pretiola*, which means "little gift." In olden times pretzels were given to children as a reward for learning their prayers. That is why the twisted shape of a pretzel is said to resemble arms folded in humble prayer.

The small Moravian town of Lititz claims the first commercial pretzel bakery in the country. In 1850 a stranger, to repay a kindness, gave a pretzel to a baker named Julius Sturgis. It became so popular that by 1861 this small bakery turned out nothing but pretzels.

Today hard pretzels are made by machine, but soft pretzels are still made by hand in Pennsylvania Dutch country. The Pennsylvania Dutch love pretzels. There is Pretzel Soup and they even serve pretzels on ice cream. Pretzels come in all shapes and sizes, and numerous pretzel factories located in Pennsylvania ship their products worldwide.

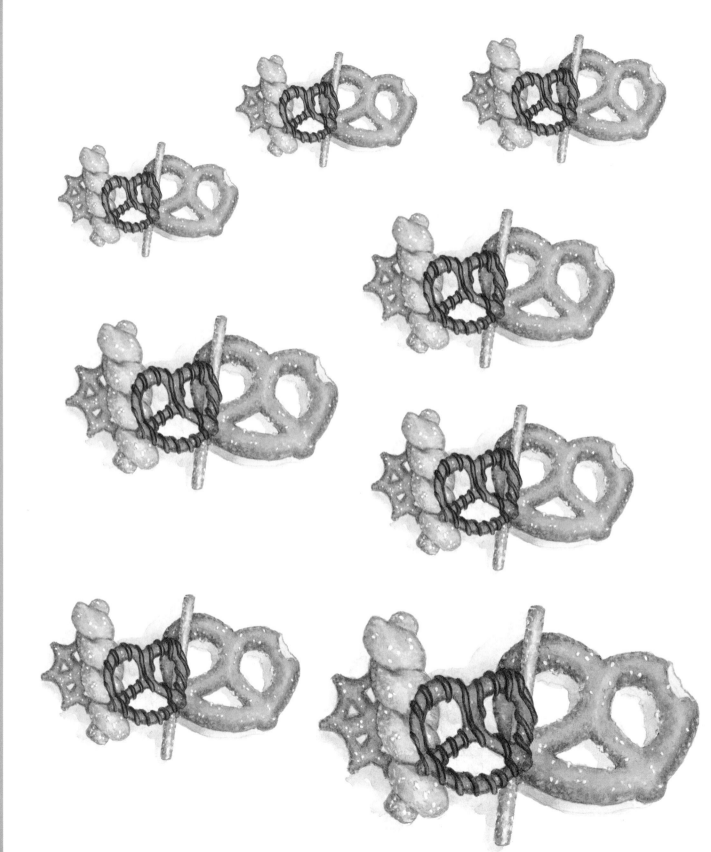

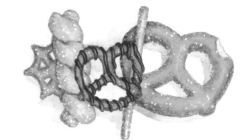

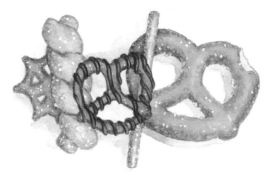

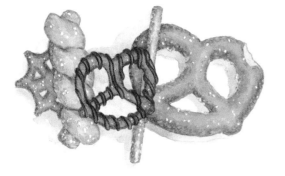

How many pretzels to make a big bunch?
How many pretzels to make a loud **crunch**?
How many pretzels can you munch with lunch?
90 pretzels is my hunch!

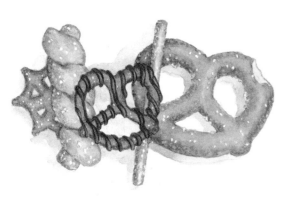
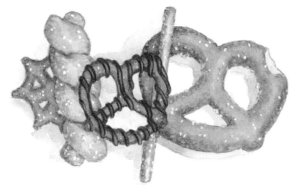
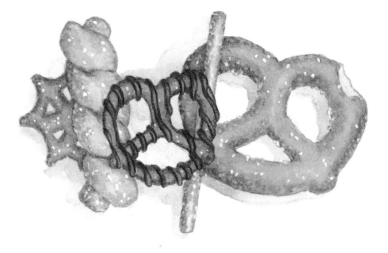

100 chocolates are so much fun,
especially when we count them one by one.
But when we finish and the count is done,
let's share this chocolate treat with everyone!

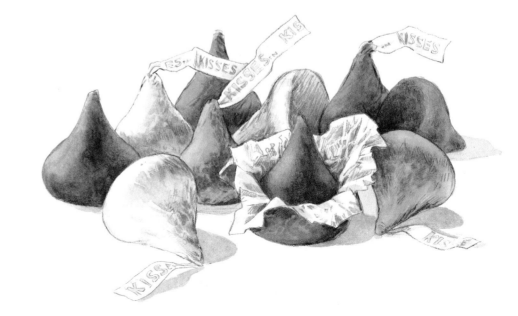

The world's largest chocolate factory is in Hershey, where the two main streets are named Chocolate and Cocoa Avenues and the streetlights are shaped like Hershey's® Kisses® Brand Chocolates.

In 1900 Milton S. Hershey built a factory in Derry Church to perfect the milk chocolate bar. He mass-produced it to keep the price down so all Americans could afford this tasty luxury. Concerned for the people who were employed by his company, Milton Hershey built a model company town, which was named in his honor. With no children of their own, Milton Hershey and his wife, Catherine, established the Hershey Industrial School in 1909, a school for orphaned boys. Today Milton Hershey School serves boys and girls pre-kindergarten through twelfth grade.

Invented in 1907, eighty million Hershey's® Kisses® Brand Chocolates are produced each day in factories located in California and Pennsylvania! Today approximately 1.5 million tourists visit Hershey each year.

one
hundred
100

Trinka Hakes Noble

Trinka Hakes Noble is the noted author of numerous award-winning picture books including *The Scarlet Stockings Spy*, an IRA Teacher's Choice 2005, illustrated by Robert Papp. Ms. Noble also wrote the ever-popular *Jimmy's Boa* series and *Meanwhile Back at the Ranch* (both featured on Reading Rainbow). Her many awards include ALA Notable Children's Book, *Booklist* Children's Editors' Choice, IRA-CBC Children's Choice, *Learning:* The Year's Ten Best, and several Junior Literary Guild Selections.

A member of the Rutgers University Council on Children's Literature, she was awarded Outstanding Woman 2002 in Arts and Letters in the state of New Jersey for her lifetime work in children's books. Ms. Noble lives in Bernardsville, New Jersey.

Lisa Papp

Born and raised in Iowa and Nebraska, Lisa Papp attended Iowa State University College of Design for one year, and studied three more years at Du Cret School for the Arts in New Jersey where she won numerous awards for her watercolor paintings. "I am lucky to illustrate. It gives me a chance to dream and see it come to life. Nature has always been a friend to me and continues to be one of my best inspirers." Lisa currently resides in historic Bucks County, Pennsylvania, with her artist husband, Rob, and their whimsical cat, Taffy.